Riot!

The Incredibly True Story of How 1,000
Prisoners Took Over Attica Prison

ABSOUTE
CRME

By Fergus Mason

Absolute Crime Books

www.absolutecrime.com

Table of Contents

About Us

Absolute Crime publishes only the best true crime literature. Our focus is on the crimes that you've probably never heard of, but you are fascinated to read more about. With each engaging and gripping story, we try to let readers relive moments in history that some people have tried to forget.

Remember, our books are not meant for the faint at heart. We don't hold back—if a crime is bloody, we let the words splatter across the page so you can experience the crime in the most horrifying way!

If you enjoy this book, please visit our homepage to see other books we offer; if you have any feedback, we'd love to hear from you!

Introduction

September 1971 was cooler than average in New York State, but that didn't apply to the temperature inside Attica Correctional Center. The hulking high-security prison was packed well past its capacity, with 2,250 prisoners jammed into blocks meant to hold only 1,200, and the strict regime common in American jails at the time was causing tension. Conditions inside Attica were appalling. Some of it was due to the superintendent's harsh policies but much was simply because the infrastructure couldn't cope with the numbers; many of the supply contracts were still based on the prison's official capacity, so each man had a monthly ration of one roll of toilet paper. Showers were restricted to one per week, and with so many men crammed into the cellblocks that made the atmosphere unpleasant in more ways than one.

The tension had risen still further since late August. On August 21 George Jackson, a Black Panther radical jailed in California's San Quentin jail, had a meeting with his lawyer in the visiting room. On the way back to his cell after the meeting a corrections officer spotted a glint of metal under Jackson's hair. He asked him what it was, and Jackson replied by pulling out a 9mm Astra semiautomatic pistol.[1] In the orgy of violence which followed four guards and two white inmates died with gunshot wounds and slit throats. It ended when Jackson was shot dead while trying to escape across the yard and out the gate. Despite the murderous rampage he'd initiated Jackson was a hero to many Attica inmates, especially the political radicals, and his death had infuriated them. Soon that fury would

---

[1] Attorney Stephen Bingham always denied having smuggled the gun into San Quentin, but immediately after the visit with Jackson he fled to Europe and didn't return to the USA for 13 years. In 1986 he was acquitted on all charges arising from the incident. It should be noted that Jackson had been strip-searched before meeting Bingham and the attorney was carrying a briefcase with a large tape recorder in it. The pistol, with its grip scales removed, was flat enough to fit inside the recorder's empty casing.

spark an even worse eruption.

Prisons can be dangerous places, especially high-security ones like Attica. When a couple of thousand people are crammed together in one place, and all of them are criminals, you can hardly expect anything else. Beatings, rape and even murder happen inside big jails. Corrections officers do a risky job and quickly learn to watch their backs. What was about to happen at Attica in September 1971 was something completely different, though. Even hardened criminals were shocked at the outpouring of rage and brutality that swept through the inmate population. On September 9, in a matter of minutes, Attica went from a strictly disciplined institution to a killing ground where death could strike anyone, at any time. The riot began with demands for better conditions that were exploited by political extremists for their own purposes. It ended in a frenzy of violence, with inmates killing inmates and guards killing guards. By the time the smoke and drifting clouds of tear gas cleared 39 men were dead, most of them slain in a hail of gunfire as the state police launched a bungled operation to take back control of the prison. Lawsuits, recriminations and compensation claims kept lawyers busy for more than 30 years and legislators are still trying to get at the whole story.

The Attica riot has been the subject of countless articles, books and movies. Most of them were based on media coverage from the time or were sensationalized versions made to push an agenda. In 2002, though, a state task force heard days of testimony from the surviving hostages and the relatives of those who died. Now it's possible to tell the story of Attica through the eyes of those who were at the heart of it.

Chapter 1: Buildup to Riot

The irony of the Attica riot is that the New York prison system was already taking steps towards reform and a more modern, rehabilitative, approach. Governor Nelson Rockefeller had ordered a commission on prison reform in 1966, and by 1970 this was starting to recommend changes in the antiquated system. For nearly 150 years US prisons had been based on the "Auburn System," which had been developed in New York in 1826 at Auburn Prison. This philosophy was based around extremely strict discipline and hard labor. The intention was to redeem prisoners by a combination of religious education, enforced contemplation of their crimes and salvation through work. In 1826 it was fairly typical of prisons worldwide; by the 1970s it was looking very out of date. Most other countries had moved to a system that attempted to rehabilitate inmates and were trying to cut down the number of people in prison, and several US states wanted to follow their example. New York was one of them. On

January 1, 1971 the Department of Correction and the Division of Parole were combined into the Department of Correctional Services, in an attempt to create a continuous system that would handle criminals from their arrest to their eventual release from prison. The Division of Probation, which had been part of the Department of Correction, was moved to the new organization's Executive Department and reformed.

The head of the new Department of Correctional Services was Russell G. Oswald, a former high school athlete, law school graduate and U.S. Navy officer who had been working in correctional departments since the early 1950s.[i] Oswald's philosophy was "no case is hopeless" and he had built a reputation as a humanitarian and dedicated prison reformer. He had already been serving on the New York State Parole Board since 1957 and was well respected by many in the legal system. He also faced opposition, however. Many prison administrators and corrections officers disagreed with Oswald's proposed reforms. They believed that relaxing discipline inside prisons would be dangerous for the staff, and that liberalizing the rules would be unpopular. Many prison administrators had political ambitions and were concerned that if they implemented better conditions inside their prisons they could be accused of "coddling" the inmates.

There was also another, more practical problem with reforming New York's overcrowded jails - there wasn't any money. New York was suffering serious financial difficulties and the correctional budget had already been slashed to the bone. Unless Oswald got more funding for his department he wouldn't be able to make any improvements to the conditions the inmates were living in. This wasn't just a matter of making the facilities more comfortable or supplying more toilet paper; to give prisoners more freedom of movement inside a jail you need to hire more staff. Unfortunately for Oswald the trend was against him; between 1967 and 1971 the correctional slice of the state budget fell from 4.8 percent to only 3.0 percent. In simple dollars it increased by $19 million, but rising prices had eaten up any effect of that and in real terms the budget was falling behind. Through the early part of 1971 Oswald managed to get an extra $8 million to spend on Attica but it wasn't anywhere near enough. The prison was nearly 40 years old and had been built to an old-fashioned design, where prisoners were expected to spend most of their time locked down in the cells.

Oswald was well aware that conditions inside Attica were explosive. The regime in the old prison was exactly what he'd spent the last 15 years campaigning against and he wanted to see it changed, but his options were limited. He did what he could though. Early reforms allowed the media more access to prisons, so the American people could get a better look at what was happening inside the walls. Inmates' mail had been routinely censored by guards, but now this was restricted so that letters should only be read where there was a genuine need to. Visiting rights were improved. Oswald also ordered the department to serve better food to prisoners. He wasn't concerned with making it more appetizing but it could certainly do with being more nutritious, and he gave catering officials permission to go over budget if that was what it took to raise standards. Another change in the kitchens was that from now on Muslim prisoners would be offered alternatives to pork.

The issue of Islamic dietary requirements was becoming a significant one in 1971. The U.S. prison population hadn't yet begun the explosive growth that started in the mid-1970s and only began slowing down slightly in 2008, but the demographics of that population were changing. An increasing percentage of inmates were black or Hispanic - 54% of those in Attica were black[ii] - and particularly among black prisoners jailhouse conversions to Islam were becoming common. Louis Farrakhan of the controversial Nation of Islam was a spiritual leader to many inmates, but there were also a large number of more mainstream Muslims among the prisoners. U.S. prisons didn't have a lot of experience when it came to prisoners with special dietary needs; the number of religious Jews in prison had always been so tiny that it was easy to make special arrangements with a local delicatessen or simply pretend the problem wasn't there. Now, though, a prison the size of Attica could contain several hundred Muslims and they weren't happy to be handed a plate of beans and franks. Providing them with suitable food would play a part in reducing tension within the prison.

The growing number of Hispanic prisoners caused problems, too. Many of them were from families where the first language was Spanish, so naturally letters from parents and wives were written in that language. Few of the guards spoke it, though, and this led to problems with censorship of incoming mail. Often letters - as well as magazines and newspapers - in Spanish were simply assumed to be contraband and went straight in the trash.[iii] For inmates whose parents spoke little English this made staying in touch with the outside world almost impossible.

Poor living conditions and over-zealous censorship weren't the only problems in Attica that summer. As well as the normal racial and religious tensions inevitable when nearly 3,000 inmates and staff are crammed into a confined space there was another factor at work - radical politics.

The Black Panther Party was formed in Oakland, California in 1966. It began as part of the widespread Black Power movement, and originally its goal was to improve the conditions of black Americans and defend their communities against the police violence that was widespread at the time. Its philosophy evolved rapidly though, and by 1971 it had cut back its emphasis on racial issues and become more of a communist revolutionary movement. Every member of the party was encouraged to read Mao's "Little Red Book" as an introduction to revolutionary tactics, and the leaders formed links with other extreme left-wing groups both in the USA and abroad.

The Panther Party is difficult to categorize. It was deeply committed to revolutionary politics and hated the authorities - especially the police - but it also spent a lot of time working on social programs. One of its early activities, beginning in January 1969, was a program to give free breakfasts to children from poor families; this started at one Oakland church but by the end of the year was feeding over 10,000 children daily in cities across America. The Panthers set up free medical clinics, rehabs for alcoholics and drug addicts and an emergency ambulance service. They were often the only ones providing these services in poor areas and they made life better for tens of thousands of people, of all races. At the same time groups of armed Panthers were following the police, allegedly to "monitor" them and watch for cases of brutality or racism. At least one group of these "monitors," led by Panther leader Eldridge Cleaver, decided to carry out some brutality of their own; on April 6 1968 they ambushed an Oakland police patrol, and 17 year old Panther Bobby Hutton was killed in the gunfight that followed. He was the first Panther to die violently, but he wasn't the last. By 1970 the Panthers had murdered 15 policemen and 34 of their own were dead, killed by the police or by other Panther factions. By the mid-1970s the conflict between various political factions and the members who were more interested in fighting the police had started to tear the organization apart, and membership nosedived. By 1980 it was down to just 27 members, and the free school started by the Panthers closed in 1982 after founder Huey Newton was caught stealing its funds to pay for his drug habit.[iv]

In 1971, though, the Black Panthers were at the height of their popularity. They were also at the height of their conflict with the police, and most big prisons had a few Panthers among the inmates. Worse, they had a lot of wannabes - gang members and other criminals who were inspired by the Panthers, but ignored the social justice aims of the movement and just enjoyed the violence. These hangers-on weren't exactly sophisticated thinkers, and a lot of them couldn't see the difference between someone who was in prison *for* their political beliefs and someone who was in prison *with* their political beliefs. The USA in 1971 could be a bad place to be poor and black, but the inmates of Attica weren't being oppressed because of their race and social class; they were being oppressed because they were convicted criminals. The harsh conditions were a result of tight budgets and an outdated correctional policy, but many inmates saw it as part of the capitalist system and began to think of themselves as political prisoners.

Staff found it harder to relate to these politicized inmates than they had with more traditional jailbirds. Up until the mid-60s the guards and the convicts they supervised shared the same value system, even if they approached it from different sides. Corrections officer Richard Fargo told his son that the old-time convicts accepted they had committed a crime and were in prison to pay for it. The new class of inner city criminals was different. They blamed society, not themselves. They "felt that if they could steal from you, if they could take your life, it was your fault."[v] This different attitude opened up a divide between staff and convicts. The guards couldn't understand how the prisoners thought; the prisoners saw the guards as part of a system that oppressed them to maintain white superiority. There were other problems too. The Department of Corrections didn't seem to have recognized the changing nature of the prison population, so they didn't give officers any training on how to deal with it. Shift policy also changed in the late 1960s. each guard was assigned to a specific company of inmates. He could get to know them, understand their issues and watch their moods. If a prisoner got bad news from home staff could help through the problem. The new system was different. Guards rotated through companies and didn't build up the same rapport with the inmates. It was an explosive combination.

On September 9, 1971 a minor fight broke out between two inmates. This isn't exactly uncommon in prisons; after all there are a lot of violent people in there. As usual the guards separated them and locked them in the isolation cells to cool down.[vi] In Attica this was pretty much a daily event and usually would have been forgotten about in a few days. This time was going to be very different.

Chapter 2: The Riot

Ron Kozlowski had started working for the Department of Corrections in 1967, but in January 1968 he went into the Army. He got out in July of 1970 after a 13-month tour in Vietnam, and after taking a few months to unwind applied for his old job back. He got lucky, he thought; not only did the Department re-hire him, he even got to keep his old employee number, so the time he'd spent in the service counted towards his retirement benefits. Now he worked in the purchasing office for the Attica metal shop. He hadn't wanted to come to work on Friday, September 9 because Sunday was his birthday, but he'd found the motivation from somewhere and dragged himself to his office in B Block. Walking through the long corridors he'd wished he hadn't bothered. He'd been working in Attica for eight months now, and had learned to read the prison's moods. Today there was something wrong. Any other day, the inmates would have been jeering and catcalling as he passed. Now it was quiet. You could have heard a pin drop, he thought.[vii]

That Thursday at around 8:00am Attica was a hive of activity. The inmates, divided into their companies, were parading for breakfast and roll call. As usual they'd been confined to their cells since the night before, and as usual the blocks were buzzing with conversations as they greeted friends and swapped news. Today, though, somebody started a rumor in Block A. The story quickly spread that the two men who'd been taken to isolation for fighting were going to be beaten by the guards as a punishment. Nobody knows who started the rumor or why. It's possible that the riot wasn't as spontaneous as many think. Thomas Fargo remembers his father Richard telling him that Attica staff had found evidence it was planned in advance.[viii]

Ray Bogart paid two dollars a week for a room in the administration block; with a wife and four children in Auburn money was tight and he didn't want to waste it on an apartment in the village. The only problem was that even when he was off shift he was still inside Attica's walls, and with the tension he could feel in the prison that wasn't pleasant. On September 9 he was on duty from 7:00am. As soon as he reached his station in A Block he was briefed about the fight the night before. Lieutenant Curtis warned the new shift to be careful; he was worried that there would be more trouble, so he told the guards not to open any doors unless they were ordered to. Bogart was sweating with nerves as he got ready to let his assigned inmates - 2 Company - out for breakfast. Every cell door on his corridor was controlled from a lock box, and his hands were slipping on the brass lock handles. In the end he managed it, and led 2 Company off for breakfast. Everything stayed under control until about 8:50am, after they'd eaten and were heading back from the mess hall. Normally the inmates were let out into the yards after breakfast, but now there was a problem. One of the 5 Company inmates who'd been put in isolation after the fight was out of his cell; the door had been unlocked by mistake.[ix] Until he knew everyone was where they were supposed to be Curtis wanted the whole company back in their cells. Now a group of them were clustered around the locked gate to A Yard complaining that they wanted out. Bogart didn't know anything about this until he arrived at the gate with 2 Company bunched up behind him, and the crowd by the gate suddenly got a lot bigger. Some of the crowd were planning to play some football in the yard and were already in protective gear. They weren't happy about being locked down and they were making it known.

Now Lieutenant Curtis tried to calm the situation. Before he could explain the lockdown, however, all hell broke loose. One of the inmates screamed a curse and punched him in the face. Bogart and the captain of A Block, Lieutenant Elmer Huehn, raced to help Curtis and managed to get him away from the gate. Bogart lost his nightstick when someone hit him on the head with a football helmet; Huehn was half-unconscious from a blow to the face. The three battered officers somehow got away from the growing riot and into A Block, where Huehn got them into a cell and locked the door. For the moment they were safe, but the chaos was spreading swiftly.

John Stockholm was leading a group of inmates from D Block back from breakfast in the dining hall when he noticed a commotion in A Corridor.[x] The main building at Attica is laid out in a hollow square. Each of the cellblocks, named A to D, forms a side. The inner space is divided into four exercise yards, also named A to D. Covered corridors separate the yards, and in the center they meet at the eight-sided command center that everyone in Attica calls Times Square. Seen from above the corridors - known as "tunnels" to staff and inmates - look like an enormous cross splitting the prison into quarters.

Stockholm was supervising between 60 and 70 inmates on his own, a difficult task but a common one in the short-staffed, overcrowded prison. He was supposed to escort them to D Yard, where they'd be free to exercise for a while before starting work. Seeing the trouble in A Corridor he stopped to evaluate the situation and work out what to do. Then a senior officer, Harry Whelan, ran up to him. Whelan was captain of D Block and he quickly explained what was going on. There were officers in A Yard and they were in trouble; inmates in the yard and up in the cellblock were pelting them with missiles - weight bars, rocks, anything that could be thrown. Whelan ordered Stockholm to attract the officers' attention and tell them to pull back, out of the yard; the situation was too dangerous and A Yard would need to be abandoned to the rioters until backup arrived. Stockholm left Whelan with the prisoners and headed off to rescue his colleagues.

Back in A Corridor a group of rioters were crowded against the gate leading into Times Square, yelling abuse at the staff sheltering behind it. So far the situation was bad but not out of control; one cellblock was in an uproar, but the staff still controlled most of the prison. If they could lock the other inmates down and isolate the affected cellblock the riot would probably fade out when people got hungry.

Suddenly a faulty bolt on the gate gave way and it swung open. The mob could now reach the corridors leading out from Times Square into the other three cellblocks, and they flooded through. Stockholm was trying without success to attract the attention of the guards in A Yard. Now he heard a sudden rush of feet behind him and started to turn, but a blow on the head with a broom handle sent him sprawling on the floor. More blows rained down on him as he lay helpless. Within seconds he was unconscious. Royal Morgan was heading down to A Corridor to see what was happening when an inmate called Plumber, who'd been transferred to Attica after instigating a riot at Auburn the year before, knocked him to the floor with a length of two by four.

The rioters now had access to every area of the main prison building and they spread out quickly. One group ran into the control room and attacked the staff there. They'd armed themselves with improvised weapons on the way and their cornered victims were savagely beaten with baseball bats, chains, lengths of timber[xi] and sections of steel pipe. One of them, William Quinn, was bludgeoned unconscious with a two by four. Later a group of inmates put his limp body on a mattress and carried him down to the gate.

Up in his office behind the paint shop Ron Kozlowski heard a whistle start up from the prison power house. Training for staff was mostly on the job back then, and he'd never been told what - if anything - the whistle meant. He left his office and went to a window that overlooked the prison yards. A few inmates were running about, but apart from that there wasn't much activity. He went back to the office and asked the other staff if they knew anything. Nobody did. The inmates working in the paint shop were milling around and Kozlowski noticed that they looked nervous,[xii] but he didn't ask them if they knew anything. They probably wouldn't have told him anyway. After a while Kozlowski heard the sounds of an approaching riot, then crashing sounds in the paint shop. Finally the office door opened and armed convicts walked in. They told the horrified staff that they had to go with them and led them to the stairs. One of them caught hold of Kozlowski's tie and used it to pull him along. As soon as he got a chance he took the tie off and threw it away before someone tried to strangle him with it. His glasses were grabbed off his nose and thrown away. As they were led through B Block he smelled smoke; parts of the block were on fire. Inmates stopped him to go through his pockets and he was robbed of his wallet, his prison key ring, even his car keys. Then they reached B Corridor, leading from the block to Times Square, and he realized just how bad the situation was.

The corridor was a hundred yards long and it was lined with inmates. Most of them were holding improvised weapons - mop handles, shovels, and lengths of two by four. It looked like a gauntlet. It was. The captured staff were told to run along it, and as soon as they did the convicts started swinging. By the time Kozlowski reached Times Square his upper body was covered in bruises, there were lumps rising on his head and his hands and arms had been pounded as he tried to block the blows that rained down on him. By now he was convinced that he was going to die. He'd survived more than a year in Vietnam, and here he was going to die in upstate New York.

He survived as far as Times Square, though. The group of captives were led through Times Square and down the corridor towards D Block, but before reaching it they were taken out into D Yard. Now another group of inmates took charge of them. They were Black Muslims, they told Kozlowski, and they were going to protect him. He had no illusions about why; "This is because they needed us later for insurance," he told an inquiry.[xiii] His new "protectors" tied his arms and legs, blindfolded him and dumped him with the other hostages. They were arranged in a circle, back to back, and a ring of Muslim prisoners surrounded them. The Muslims wanted them for insurance; hundreds of other inmates just wanted them dead.

Not all the inmates felt that way. Royal Morgan had already been forced to strip by one group of inmates, and was being beaten by another who'd caught him trying to help William Quinn. Then a convict named Rodriguez turned up wearing a football helmet and carrying a hammer. "Leave him alone, he's mine, I want him," he told Morgan's attackers. Morgan remembered locking him up the month before and now he expected revenge. What he got was a surprise. "Mr. Morgan, I'll get you out of here or I'll hide you," Rodriguez said.[xiv] He led Morgan to a cell and showed him how to jam the door shut with a baseball bat. He also tried to find some clothes for him, but couldn't get any in his size. Morgan spent a couple of hours barricaded in the cell wishing he was back in Vietnam, until a group of inmates managed to sneak him and four other staff down to the gate and freedom. This was probably the same group who'd got Quinn out.

Huehn, Curtis and Bogart had no such luck. Some rioters had found them in the cell, but wandered off again when they realized the door was locked and couldn't be opened. Now they came back with a five-gallon gas can and told Huehn that if he didn't come out they were going to burn him. Then another inmate who he recognized promised that if they surrendered and opened the door they wouldn't be harmed. Huehn knew there was no choice; they were now trapped, and if the gasoline was poured into their cell there would be no escape. He opened the door and the three of them were led down to the yard.

Meanwhile, outside Attica, things were happening. Guards had sounded the alarm and the response was swift. New York State Police units raced to the prison and set up a perimeter to prevent a mass breakout. With the outside of the wall secure they moved in and attempted to take back control of the jail itself. The State Police were armed with pump action shotguns and tear gas grenades, and they entered the prison in force. The inmates only had two gas grenade launchers taken from guards, and they fell back in the face of superior firepower. By about 10:30am, barely two hours after the riot started, the police had regained control of two of the four cellblocks and forced the rioters back into D Yard and cellblocks B and D.

And then they stopped. The rioters had been surrounded and confined in one section of the jail, and the sensible thing for them to do now was to surrender and end the affair with as little bloodshed as possible. Sensible people weren't in charge, though. The rebelling inmates collected in D Yard and they brought their hostages with them. In total they had abducted 40 guards and civilian staff and now they played their ace; they threatened to kill the hostages if the state police didn't back off. The captives were blindfolded and penned in at the center of the yard, surrounded by a low barrier made of wooden benches, and a group of inmates armed with knives and clubs ringed them to prevent any escape attempt.

The rioters were basically in a trap, surrounded by a 35 foot wall and overlooked by the high guard towers built in to all four corners of the prison. As long as they had so many captives, though, they were secure enough for the moment. Now the ringleaders' thoughts turned to how they could take advantage of the situation. The current standoff couldn't last forever; it had to end within the next few days and the prisoners wanted to gain something from it. They put together a list of demands they wanted the authorities to meet. Much of it was pretty reasonable, and covered issues that had been discussed between inmates and administration before the riot. Demands included improved living conditions, increased religious freedom, an end to censorship of mail and more access to telephone calls. As Oswald wanted to make progress on all those issues there was common ground there, and if the inmates had left it at that the riot might have ended very differently.

There was one more demand, though, and it was obvious from the start that it was going to be difficult for the authorities to accept - they wanted an amnesty, a guarantee that none of them would face charges for their actions during the riot. The damage to the prison could have been overlooked, but staff had been viciously assaulted and hostages had been taken. Worst of all, William Quinn was now in hospital in a critical condition; at the very least that was battery with intent, and the way Quinn looked it could become murder. Granting an amnesty to crimes as serious as that could set a very dangerous precedent. It's easy to understand why the inmates wanted an amnesty, because without it some of them could be looking at a life sentence on top of whatever they were already serving, but it cast a serious shadow on the negotiations.

Chapter 3: Negotiations

News of the riot spread slowly out from the prison. Thomas Fargo was in his first week of seventh grade at Attica Junior High. Already he was used to the whistle on the prison's power house; it sounded regularly, whenever an inmate walked off his assigned area on the prison farm. On September 9, though, it kept going. Then smoke began to rise above the high walls of the jail. Slowly it sank in that a riot was under way inside the jail. Frightened of a mass escape attempt, teachers cancelled all outdoor activities and the students stayed inside the school as the volunteer fire department's truck raced past in the direction of the prison. Many of the students had fathers working in there - like Thomas's father Richard - and they were worried. They weren't the only ones. News of the uprising was causing something close to panic in the state government.

Attica is a state prison, so it comes under the authority of the Governor of New York. In 1971 this was Nelson Aldrich Rockefeller, a popular Republican who'd been in office since 1959. Rockefeller was the grandson of Standard Oil founder John D. Rockefeller, and was a prominent member of his immensely wealthy and influential family. He was educated at the Lincoln School, the prestigious Phillips Exeter Academy and finally Dartmouth College; he graduated in 1930 and immediately started a career in the family's diverse businesses. Among other jobs he worked at Chase National Bank, the Rockefeller Center and Standard Oil's Venezuelan subsidiary, Creole Petroleum. As well as his business activities, though, he also took an interest in public office. His first government position was as a member of the Westchester County Board of Health, which he joined in 1933 and stayed with for the next 20 years. In 1940 Franklin D. Roosevelt appointed him as a special representative to counter Nazi influence in Latin America, which had large communities with German roots. Later, in 1944, he became Assistant Secretary of State for American Republic Affairs.

In 1956 Rockefeller resigned from federal service so he could concentrate his attention on New York politics. He spent the next two years working on committees that were trying to simplify the state constitution. For anyone interested in running for office this was the perfect way to get a crash course in NY state politics; dozens of meetings and discussions taught him every detail of how the state government worked, and also gave him introductions to all the key political figures. When the 1958 election for state governor came round Rockefeller stood, and easily defeated incumbent W. Averell Harriman despite the Democrats having a good year almost everywhere else in the country. He was re-elected in 1962, 1966 and 1970 and proved to be a very popular governor. He was firmly on the moderate wing of the Republican Party; in fact he was so strongly identified as a moderate that the left wing of the party came to be known as "Rockefeller Republicans." During his long run as governor he passed many laws against racial and sexual discrimination, pushed the state to ratify the Civil Rights Amendment, increased the number of black state employees by nearly 50 percent and implemented a state minimum wage. He was also tough on law and order, though; under his administration the state police doubled in size and was given new stop and search powers. Rockefeller's politics were a complex mixture that would make him instinctively sympathetic to many of the inmates' demands, but extremely hostile to their actions.

Now Rockefeller was being confronted with a list of demands that made his political antennae twitch. The points about living conditions were fair ones; he'd agreed with and supported Oswald's attempts to make life better inside the state's jails. The prisoners wanted Attica transferred to federal control. That wasn't very realistic, and it could be taken as a criticism of the Department of Correctional Services, but there wasn't anything unreasonable about it. Calls for the replacement of Attica's superintendent were only to be expected, and something could be done about that if a compromise solution turned out to be possible. There were wider-reaching political concerns, though. Rockefeller focused on the language the prisoners had used in their announcement. Phrases like "unmitigated oppression," "racist administrative network" and "ruthless brutalization… throughout the Unites States"[xv] had a revolutionary ring to them. Rockefeller quickly became convinced that the instigators of the riot were radicals from the Black Panthers or a like-minded organization. His fear was that climbing down to the rioters' demands would spark a wave of similar incidents across the country. The financial cost alone would be huge, many lives would certainly be lost, and there would be a risk of mass escapes that could put hundreds of murderers back on the streets. Moderate as he was, Rockefeller decided that he had to take a tough line on Attica.

The big question was who would negotiate on behalf of the state. The inmates demanded that Rockefeller himself go to the prison to talk to them. Rockefeller didn't think that was a good idea; he sent an aide instead and headed off to the family estate at Pocantico Hills. With the governor having ruled himself out, Oswald put together a negotiating team that took in the Corrections Department, state politicians and the media. Other people were also attracted by the negotiations and played a role, not always with the approval of Oswald. Here are some of the main players in the talks with the inmates:

- Robert Douglass was Rockefeller's counsel and secretary from 1965 to 1972. When the siege began Rockefeller asked him to monitor the situation from his office in Albany. Later, when negotiations began to break down, he sent him to the prison as his personal representative.

- State Senator John R. Dunne was a lawyer and moderate Republican politician, and in 1971 was chairman of the Senate Corrections Committee. From the start of the process he was critical of Rockefeller's decision to stay away.

- State Representative Arthur Eve was a Democrat who, like Dunne, had been elected to the New York State Legislature in 1966. An Army veteran, he had been involved in the civil rights movement since the 1950s and was one of the first (and most respected) black politicians to come to prominence in New York State.

- Tom Wicker was an editor at the New York Times. He had a keen interest in politics and regularly wrote columns about both state and national government. He was an opponent of racial segregation and supported the civil rights movement.

He also earned a place on Nixon's "enemies list."

- William Kunstler described himself as a radical lawyer and spent most of the 1960s and 1970s working on civil rights cases. In 1971 he was a director of the ACLU and had recently defended eight anti-war campaigners indicted for causing riots in Chicago. One of them was Black Panther founder Bobby Seale.

- Louis Farrakhan, previously Louis X, previously Louis Wolcott, was an influential member of the Nation of Islam (which he now leads.) This movement, founded in 1934, draws most of its membership from black Americans. It's a mix of Islam and radical Black Power politics, which is widely described as a hate group and is deeply unpopular with mainstream Muslims. Farrakhan's mentor in the organization was Malcolm X, who was expelled in 1964 and became a conventional Muslim. The Nation of Islam got a high percentage of its converts from prisons.

Oswald went into the yard on Friday September 10 to negotiate with the inmates. At that point there was a list of 31 demands, mostly to do with living conditions inside the prison. Douglass was relaying the progress of the negotiations back to Rockefeller and felt quite optimistic. Oswald was explaining to the inmates that he was working on reforms that would meet many of their demands, and despite the difficult atmosphere of the negotiations - they were taking part with nearly 1,300 prisoners looking on, many of them hostile - it seemed to be going down well. There was only one glitch - the inmates were asked to confirm that all 42 of their hostages were alive and well.

By revealing how many staff they believed were being held the authorities had made a mistake. The inmates were only holding 40 captives. They quickly realized that the number of hostages they had was two short of what Oswald *thought* they had. Somewhere in the prison two officers were on the loose. In fact they were being sheltered by prisoners who didn't agree with the hostage taking.

John Stockholm had been knocked unconscious early in the riot, and a group of inmates had carried him to a cell in D Block. When he came round they took his shirt and gave him a gray prison one to wear, then told him to hide under the bed. They told Stockholm that they would try to get him out when things calmed down. For a day Stockholm remained hidden under the bed, narrowly avoiding discovery when a prisoner came into the cell to collect a typewriter from a locker. As the man bent to open the locker his head came within 18 inches of Stockholm's, but his attention was all on the locker and he didn't look under the bed.

Now the inmates who'd hidden him came back to the cell and pulled Stockholm out. They explained to him that the rioters were going through the cellblock, searching for him cell by cell. They were frightened of what would happen if he was caught hiding and had decided that he'd be safer with the hostages in the yard. Now they told him they would cause a disturbance and, when he heard it, he should come out of the cell and get to the end of the block. The group would then try to get him to the yard without him being beaten by the rioters. Stockholm waited until he heard the shouting start down the corridor, then he emerged from his hiding place. On the gallery he found fellow officer Art Smith, the first he'd known that he was there. It turned out later that Smith had known Stockholm was in the next cell, but Stockholm had thought he was alone. With the two of them out of the cells they were blindfolded and led down to join the hostages in D Yard.

The hostages were, for now, being protected by the Black Muslims. Many of the inmates themselves were in a much worse position. Channel Two journalist Stewart Dan and his cameraman had been allowed in to the yard on Thursday and Friday to cover the early negotiation sessions. The rioters had been watching Dan's reports and were so pleased that when he was late arriving on Saturday they insisted the negotiators wait until he got there before talks started. Dan was reporting honestly on conditions inside the prison, but now he got a chilling glimpse of what the rioters were capable of. He was talking to two inmates, Hess and Schwartz, about how the riot had got started when one of the leaders came over to see what was going on. Hess and Schwartz were taken away by a group of prisoners and Dan was assured that they were just being isolated because they were suspected informers. They'd be OK, he was told, they just weren't welcome around the negotiations. When the riot was over

Hess and Schwartz were both dead, their throats cut by fellow convicts.

Outside the prison there was some confusion. Mary Stockholm, anxiously waiting for news of her husband, heard a rumor that two hostages had been released. One of her friends went to Attica to check. When he returned he had to tell her that the reports were false and Stockholm and Smith were now in the yard with the others. For Mary this was worse than if he had been captured at the beginning; she was worried that there would be reprisals against the two officers and the prisoners who had hidden them.[xvi]

Meanwhile the negotiations went on and it looked like real progress was being made. Between Oswald and the inmates they had reached agreement on 28 of the demands. Douglass reported back to Rockefeller that there didn't seem to be any problems and everything was being sorted out. District Attorney Lewis James wrote a letter to the rioters stating that there would be no mass prosecutions for the events of the riot; he would only prosecute inmates where there was good evidence against a specific individual.

Then, on Saturday September 11, William Quinn died. His death was announced almost immediately. The inmates quickly heard about it on the news, which they were watching on a TV in the yard. Oswald hadn't agreed to an amnesty yet, and in fact he couldn't; not even the governor had the power to do that. Rockefeller could issue pardons, but only after someone had been tried and convicted. The demand for an amnesty had been a sticking point in the negotiations because it wasn't in anyone's power to give one, and now that left some of the inmates facing a possible murder charge. Douglass assured the rioters that there would be no indiscriminate persecutions once the riot ended; if Quinn's killers could be identified they would be prosecuted, but there wouldn't be blanket charges against everyone. A deal was reached and the inmate leaders went off to discuss it with other prisoners. They didn't come back with an agreement, though; they came back with more demands. This time there was no chance of an agreement.

The letter from District Attorney James was ripped up by the rioters[xvii] and the demand for an amnesty was repeated. It had to be a total amnesty - nobody was to be charged with Quinn's murder. That was clearly unacceptable. The precedent it would set was appalling; if it went through, all any future murderer would have to do to get off would be take some hostages and threaten to kill them unless he was given amnesty. There was no way this could be granted even if an amnesty was possible. The second demand wasn't much better. The rioters wanted to be flown to political asylum in a "non-imperialist country." In the language of revolutionaries that was code for a communist state. Given the widespread fears about communist radicalism a demand like that wasn't going to help their case. It just seemed to confirm Rockefeller's worries that the riot had been instigated by revolutionaries. The chances of it being granted were slim. Douglass had the feeling that the convicts knew this; they were deliberately making impossible demands to force a confrontation. The rest of the negotiating team agreed with him. Frustrated, they walked out of the prison to report back to the governor. On the way out they passed growing barricades.

In Cellblock D and the yard the prisoners were preparing for a fight. Ron Kozlowski was taking the chance to look around whenever he was untied and led to the restroom. At least some of the inmates were getting ready to resist if the state tried to retake the prison. Kozlowski could see barriers going up at the access points into the yard, and convicts were making weapons. From the metal shop he could hear grinders running; somebody was sharpening blades. The atmosphere was deteriorating too. On Friday and Saturday everyone's attention had been on the negotiations. Now those seemed to have collapsed and tempers were rising. Right from the start of the siege the hostages had been aware that some inmates just wanted to kill them. It was terrifying to sit there, bound and blindfolded, and listen to the scuffles around the ring of Muslim prisoners, the shouts of "I'm gonna kill a pig." Now it was getting worse. As darkness fell on Sunday night the tension in the yard was unbelievable. Hardly anyone slept. It had been raining on and off all day and despite the crude shelters they'd built in the yard everyone was wet and uncomfortable. The inmates now believed that an assault would be coming soon, and it would be time to use the hostages.

Chapter 4: Retaking the prison

Whenever hostages are being held it's standard practice to have a rescue plan in place. It's impossible to tell when or why negotiations might break down; hostage takers aren't famously rational, after all, and they've already crossed the line of using human lives as a bargaining chip. When hostages start dying there's usually no choice but to storm the location and save as many of the captives as possible. What happens to the hostage takers when the assault goes in depends on the laws the rescue force are operating under, but it's generally accepted that anyone close to the hostages with a weapon is a legitimate target.

By Monday morning it was obvious the negotiations weren't going anywhere. A group of the prisoners now decided it was time to use the hostages to apply a little pressure. Eight of the captives were taken up on top of one of the catwalks and sat on wooden chairs; inmates with knives, spears and clubs stood beside them, threatening to slit their throats. Down in D Yard more armed convicts crowded closer to the remaining hostages. When Oswald was told about this he decided that his options had run out. There could be no backing down on the demand for an amnesty, and experience shows that once hostage takers start killing their victims they don't stop. Later he said "On a much smaller scale, I think I have some feeling now of how Truman must have felt when he decided to drop the A-bomb."[xviii] There was no choice though. Oswald, the dedicated prison reformer, ordered the State Police to get ready to storm Attica. He called Rockefeller to tell him his decision. Rockefeller agreed.

The decision to end the siege with an assault was undoubtedly a good one. The way that assault was carried out, however, was stunningly incompetent. Breaking a hostage situation needs a SWAT team at least, and special forces troops are the best option. The state troopers assembled in Attica didn't have the specialist training or weapons needed for the job. The serving and former corrections officers mixed in with them were even worse; not only were they completely untrained for a task like this, they were far too emotionally involved. Rockefeller had been briefed about that by Douglass and Oswald, and he knew the implications. He ordered that the Attica guards were not to be part of the assault, except two who would go in with the state police to identify the hostages if required.

The assault force wasn't just made up of unsuitable personnel; many of them had unsuitable weapons, too. The marksmen covering the yard had .270-caliber rifles with telescopic sights, which were at least accurate and precise. The problem was they were also high powered, and that was dangerous when firing into a crowded space - bullets could easily go right through the target and kill one or two people behind him. The marksmen had been issued with expanding ammunition that they hoped would stay in the target. The State Police and corrections officers were even more of a problem. Many just had their sidearms, and pistols are notoriously inaccurate except at point blank range. The others were carrying pump action shotguns loaded with buckshot. These would fire nine or twelve .30 caliber lead balls with each shot, and while the missiles wouldn't spread much the guns were barely more accurate than a handgun. Worse, some of the shotguns were loaded with rifled slug, a single massive .729-inch projectile. These were ideal for blowing open locked doors but extremely dangerous to fire around hostages. They had the power of a rifle bullet combined with the inaccuracy of a shotgun - a lethally inappropriate combination. Some of the corrections officers who were there had brought guns from home. Others had drawn weapons - including at least one Thompson submachine gun - from the prison armory, against regulations and Rockefeller's order.

Not long after first light on September 13 Army helicopters appeared near the prison. They flew in circles around the area, constantly in motion. Some of them were too heavy to hover; they were loaded with containers of water as emergency firefighting supplies, because the inmates had gasoline in the yard and there were signs they were planning to burn some of the hostages. Not all of them were carrying water, though. At least two were loaded with canisters of gas. Some of them were CN, a commonly used tear gas that's almost identical to Mace. Others were filled with CS, an irritant developed by the British military. As well as making victims' eyes sting and water CS causes uncontrollable coughing and a burning sensation on exposed skin.

As the helicopters orbited overhead State Police commander Major John Monahan was briefing his force of 500 troopers. Monahan was concerned at the risk of casualties. There were believed to be 1,281 inmates and 42 hostages in D Yard and the dangers of shooting down into it were obvious. He reminded the men of the laws about use of firearms. State troopers are only allowed to fire their weapons if they believe the target is an imminent threat to life, and that rule was to be applied during the assault. Monahan didn't want a military-style onslaught on the prison - if possible he wanted it to be done with the minimum of casualties. He knew it couldn't be completely bloodless, because there were over a dozen armed inmates up on the catwalk with the hostages and they were going to have to be shot, but he hoped that volley of aimed shots would be the beginning and end of the killing.

Minutes later the assault force was moving into position. The inmates controlled Blocks B and D, so the rescue force assembled in A and C. When the assault was launched they would move along the catwalks that ran on top of A and C Tunnels, and through the tunnels themselves, until they reached Times Square. The main force of troopers on A Catwalk would be followed by a second group, which had three ladders to get down into D Yard. From there troopers would move across the yard to the hostage circle in the middle where the captives waited, bound and penned in by the wooden benches. The plan was already being subverted, though. Several of the Attica guards had joined the catwalk assault groups despite Rockefeller's orders, and they were armed. Nobody wanted to send them away when their comrades were being held hostage.

Up on the catwalk the eight hostages selected to be killed were having a hard time. Their captors were forcing them to shout "I do not want to die." Ron Kozlowski was being held by two inmates. Every time a helicopter circled near one of them would turn him, using his body as a human shield. A prisoner started shouting at Kozlowski, telling him he couldn't wait to kill him. Kozlowski asked why. "I'm not even a corrections officer," he said, "I'm a civilian." The convict had an answer for that. "You're white, ain't you?" Then he went back to taunting his victim, telling him he was going to cut his throat and pull his tongue out the wound to make a necktie.[xix] Next he brushed Kozlowski's hair, saying he wanted him to die pretty.

To the observers in the towers it was clear that things were moving rapidly towards a crisis. The inmates weren't backing down, and the governor wasn't going to pardon them all and fly them to Havana or Hanoi. They would probably start killing hostages within minutes. Now Oswald gave the order to go and the assault began.

Two of the circling helicopters broke away and raced for the prison. They came over the roof of A Block at low level and turned towards D Yard, noses coming up as they quickly lost speed and moved out over the yard at walking pace. The doors were already open; now the canisters started falling, spewing dense white clouds of tear gas and tiny crystals of hot CS. The downdraft from the rotors helped the gas spread rapidly through the whole yard. As the helicopters started their run the marksmen in A and C Blocks took aim at the convicts threatening the hostages on the catwalk. Instantly it all started to go wrong.

In movies the hero can pick up a rifle and fire it accurately. In real life it's a bit more complicated. No two people hold a gun and look through the sights exactly the same way, so to hit what you're aiming at it's essential to zero it - adjust the sights to suit your personal technique. If you don't do that the path of the bullet won't exactly match the sight line, and the impact can be a good way off what you're aiming at. The sharpshooters hadn't been given a chance to zero their rifles, so not all of them were hitting their targets. With convicts and hostages so close together it was only a matter of time before the wrong people got hit. Some of the shots were accurate; the hostage takers on the catwalk roof started to fall as bullets ripped into them. Others were going wild. Stray .270 high velocity rounds began to crack into the hostage circle. Some found victims on the roof. Two of the hostages on the catwalk were Michael Smith and John D'Arcangelo. Rifle fire from the troopers cut down the inmates threatening them

- Robert Hannigan was holding a homemade spear at Smith's stomach when a bullet from A Block killed him - but as D'Arcangelo tried to crawl under the catwalk railing and drop down to the relative safety of the yard another shot hit him in the abdomen and severed his spine. He died almost instantly.

On the catwalk the inmates were reacting to the gas and incoming fire. Kozlowski, still blindfolded, felt something hit his throat. Then the inmate holding him was gone and he dropped to the deck of the catwalk, curling into a ball in a desperate effort to avoid the storm of gunfire. Chips of cement sprayed him as wild rounds blasted the area.

As the sharpshooters opened fire the state police began advancing along the catwalks and tunnels. The rioters had set up barricades to slow down any assault but it wasn't enough to stop the troopers; they hauled some of the junk aside and scrambled over the remains. In A Tunnel State Police Captain George Rooney had briefed his men. They wouldn't be facing organized resistance, he told them, so keep control. They did. Rooney managed to lead his group the length of A Tunnel and right into the center of the prison without any of them having to fire a shot; the inmates saw them coming and backed off.

Among the other three groups, however, discipline was already breaking down. In C Tunnel the troopers were advancing in ranks with pump shotguns up front. Eyewitnesses later said it was like British colonial troops - the front rank would fire their shotguns into the clouds of gas that were pouring into the tunnels, then the next rank would come up and fire. They advanced in a constant hail of lead pellets. Later the tunnel had to be repaired because so many stray shots had scarred the inside of it.[xx] The rule about only firing where there was a threat to life had gone out the window. On A Catwalk Kenneth Malloy was lying on the deck; two troopers emptied their pistols into him. James Robinson had been shot through the lungs by one of the sharpshooters and was dying on C Catwalk, and another trooper killed him with a shotgun blast to the neck.

On the catwalks, armed corrections officers were firing indiscriminately at anything in a gray shirt. Hostage John Monteleone was killed by a shot in the chest from a Ruger .44 Magnum carbine. The rifle was privately owned by an officer who'd brought it with him. Later he said he'd been shooting at the barricade. Monteleone, a civilian worker from the metal shop, was 70 feet away from it. Michael Smith was trying to get away from the carnage when another officer opened fire on him with a submachine gun, hitting him four times in the stomach. Amazingly he survived. He was one of the lucky ones. Down in the yard three hostages had been killed by stray bullets from the marksmen and three more were injured, including metal shop supervisor Robert Van Buren who had a bullet in his hip.

Others were suffering at the hands of the rioters. Fred Miller had been forced to stand in the yard away from the other hostages. When the gas started coming down a convict hit him on the head with a lead mallet, shattering his skull and compressing fragments against his brain. He suffered permanent neurological damage. Lying on the ground semi-conscious, he heard someone ask, "Should I hit him again?" Someone else answered, "No, he's dead." Miller pretended he was. He didn't have to keep up the act for long, because the troopers had finally broken through the barricades on the catwalks and the rescue team was down in the yard. Lieutenant Joe Christian was the first man down the ladder. He was carrying his shotgun and had two pistols in his belt; he planned to give them to the hostages so they could defend themselves from any last-minute murder attempts. Half way to the hostage circle an inmate stood up and hit him over the head. Christian's helmet saved him from serious injury but the blow staggered him.

One of the troopers with him used the butt of his shotgun to knock the attacker down and they carried on towards the hostages. Then the air around them erupted in a new storm of fire.

A group of state troopers had made it to B Catwalk, and they opened up at Christian's attacker. Now the inaccuracy of the shotguns took a disastrous toll. Inmate Tommy Hicks, who was probably the one who hit Christian, died with five buckshot pellets in him but far more of the lead balls were going wild. Christian staggered again as a pellet hit his arm, then went down when a rifle bullet blew a chunk out of his calf muscle. More shotgun fire sprayed around and over him and tore into the hostage circle. In seconds five hostages were dead or dying. Ed Cunningham was killed by a single ball of buckshot that went through his cheek and out the back of his neck. Others were wounded. Walter Zimoski was hit through both lungs by a pellet that somehow missed his heart. Around the circle inmates were dying and being wounded, too, but the worst effect of the shotgun fire was on the hostages. Ballistics experts later calculated that a hostage had been *fifteen times* more likely to get shot than an inmate.

Finally the rescue party reached the hostage circle and the firing started to die down. Some troopers were still out for revenge, though. Ramon Rivera and another inmate were hiding in a hole dug under the edge of the yard. One of the troopers who'd killed Kenneth Molloy stuck the muzzle of his shotgun down the hole and fired a round. Rivera caught the blast in one leg and bled out through a severed femoral artery. Sam Melville was one of the real revolutionaries in Attica. Better known by his nickname "The Mad Bomber," he'd carried out a one-man terrorist campaign in 1969, setting off at least eight blasts and injuring 19 people. He was finally caught trying to blow up National Guard trucks and sent to Attica. It's widely suspected that he was one of the main instigators of the riot. Now he was skulking in one of the bunkers the inmates had dug. As the firing tapered off he climbed out; a state trooper leveled his shotgun and fired a rifled slug through Melville's chest.

Sam Melville was one of the last to die. Finally the sound of gunshots died away. There were nearly 1,300 inmates penned in the yard, many of them wounded, and the surviving hostages were still bound and blindfolded in the wreckage of the circle. There were hundreds of improvised weapons scattered around the yard and far too many prisoners to search. Instead they were shepherded through to A Yard and ordered to strip. That was probably a relief for many of them, because anyone who'd been caught by the CS canisters now had millions of tiny irritant crystals in their clothes. Fresh air helps clear the crystals from the skin.

What wasn't a relief was the treatment some of the corrections officers and troopers started dealing out. At the start of the riot staff had been forced to run a gauntlet and beaten by inmates; now the tables were turned and the naked prisoners were kicked and clubbed by a double rank of officers as they moved down A Corridor. Out in the yard one was forced to hold a football under his chin and threatened with death of he let it fall.

Back in D Yard state troopers and National Guard medics sorted through the dead and wounded who littered the gas-shrouded field. Fred Miller's head was wrapped in a towel and he was rushed to hospital. Ron Kozlowski was already in an ambulance with John Stockholm and Art Smith when he realized that his throat had been half cut before a marksman's bullet saved him; the blow he'd felt up on the catwalk had been a knife, and he needed 38 stitches to close the vicious wound. He was still one of the lucky ones. Nine hostages and 29 inmates had died during the assault. Four more inmates had already been murdered by the rioters and William Quinn had died two days before. In all the riot had cost 42 lives. Another 89 people were wounded.

Chapter 5: Retaliation

The rioters had had their day in the sun, but it was finally over and they were back under the control of the Attica guards. Those guards were angry. Ten of their colleagues were dead - an eleventh would die a year later - and many more injured, and they blamed the inmates. The violence of the assault hadn't been enough to work off their rage, and now they could make the inmates suffer. Beatings continued for several days, spurred on by rumors that several of the dead hostages had died of cut throats.

It wasn't just the guards who wanted revenge for the events at Attica, though. The Weather Underground Organization was an offshoot of the extreme left wing Students for a Democratic Society (SDS.) The SDS began to fall apart in 1968 and was dissolved in 1969, but one of its many squabbling factions - the Revolutionary Youth Movement - morphed into the Weathermen and remained active until 1981, although it too had begun to disintegrate in 1976 after the end of the Vietnam War. The Weathermen were motivated by opposition to what they saw as U.S. imperialism and support for what they called "national liberation movements," such as the North Vietnamese Communist Party.[2] The organization had contacts with the governments of Cuba, North Vietnam and China, and also had links with the Black Panther Party. Although most of its

[2] Ironically, when the North Vietnamese Army captured the city of Hué during the 1968 Tet Offensive the city's student radicals were some of the first victims among the estimated 6,000 citizens they murdered.

members were middle-class white leftists it strongly supported the Black Power movement. Like the Panthers the Weathermen believed that it was possible to launch a popular revolution to overthrow the U.S. government and establish a socialist republic in its place. While the Panthers spent much of their time and resources on social programs, though, the Weathermen concentrated almost exclusively on terrorism.

The first attack by the Weathermen was an attack on the Haymarket Police Memorial in Chicago, which they blew up on October 7, 1969. This was the opening move in the "Days of Rage" campaign of October 8-11, four days of rioting organized by the Weathermen and the fast-collapsing SDS in an attempt to spark widespread opposition to the war in Vietnam. On February 16 1970 a Weather Underground nail bomb exploded at a police station in San Francisco's Upper Haight neighborhood, an area strongly associated with the protest movement and 1960s counterculture. A police officer was killed in the explosion and another lost an eye. On the 21st of the same month the home of a New York judge was attacked with Molotov cocktails; the intended victim, State Supreme Court Justice Murtagh, was presiding over the trial of 21 Panthers who had been planning to bomb New York landmarks. The same night more firebombs were thrown at a police car in Brooklyn and two Manhattan military recruiting offices.

The WUO had an active bomb-making cell in New York, but it wasn't a very competent one. On March 6 there was what the British Army call an "own goal." A bomb went off in a townhouse in Greenwich Village, and when the smoke cleared the bomb squad found the mangled bodies of three Weathermen members among the wreckage. They had a better bomber available at the time though - Sam Melville. The Mad Bomber liked to operate independently but he didn't mind blowing things up for the Weathermen or Panthers either. Perhaps his death in Attica helped spur the group to get revenge.

The Weathermen received a boost on December 4, 1969 when the Chicago police raided a Black Panther safe house looking for a stockpile of weapons. In the raid two Panthers were shot dead and seven other wounded. All the evidence pointed towards massively excessive force used by the police; one of the dead Panthers was an armed guard inside the front door, but the other fatality and all the wounded were shot in bed. In response to this incident the Weathermen issued a "declaration of war" on the United States government on May 21, 1970. Its members went underground, adopting fake identities. On June 9 a bomb went off at the NYC police headquarters and the Weathermen claimed responsibility for the first time. In September they branched out into contract jobs; LSD enthusiast Timothy Leary had escaped from a low security prison in California and the Weathermen were paid $25,000 to smuggle him out of the USA.

The Weathermen had upped the stakes with their declaration of war, but they were also having membership problems. Many of them had signed on because they'd been swept up in the general wave of student radicalism that affected America at the time. A lot of them weren't too sure they wanted to risk being blown up by a home-made bomb or shot in a police raid. These less committed revolutionaries drifted back to mainstream protests and left the hard core of the movement to get on with it. As their numbers fell the Weathermen went quiet for a while, but they continued to build links with other revolutionary movements, including the Black Panther Party.

The causes of the Attica riot were pretty unremarkable - jailhouse violence, low budgets and poor living conditions - but in the atmosphere of the time it looked like a white against black issue. Outside the walls it was seized on as part of the cause, another skirmish in the approaching revolution. The Weathermen, with their close ties to Black Power, were among those who jumped on the bandwagon. They wanted to target Oswald. Of course Oswald was a dedicated prison reformer, but to the Weathermen that didn't matter a whole lot. They were motivated more by hatred of the U.S. system than anything else - their opposition to the Vietnam War didn't extend to the Northern invasion of South Vietnam, for example - and Oswald was part of that system. They decided to bomb his headquarters, the Department of Corrections in Albany. At 7:30pm on September 17 six sticks of dynamite went off close to Oswald's office.

Chapter 6: Lawsuits

Because no amnesty had been agreed to there was nothing to stop the authorities from indicting inmates for crimes committed during the riot, and they had a list of names ready. Over 60 inmates were charged with a range of offences, including the murder of William Quinn. One state policeman was also charged with reckless endangerment for his actions during the assault. The most serious charge was the murder of William Quinn. In 1975 John B. Hill, also known as John Boncore, was found guilty of murdering Quinn by beating him with a length of lumber. He was sentenced to a minimum of 20 years but pardoned, along with seven other inmates, in 1976.

The surviving hostages were assured that New York State and the Corrections Department would take care of them. They were told to take as much time off as they needed, and only to return to work when they were ready. Pay checks kept arriving while they pulled themselves back together, but what they weren't told was that those checks contained money from worker's compensation payments. By accepting the payments they gave up the right to sue the state for the conduct of the assault and the injuries many of them had suffered during it. The only exception was Linda Jones, who refused to cash the checks for her widow's pension and successfully sued New York.

Already bitter at being denied the right to sue, the survivors were outraged when a group of inmates and relatives launched a class action suit against the state for civil rights violations. The case dragged on for well over a decade, but in 2000 the State of New York agreed to pay $8 million to the families of inmates killed as well as to some of those who had been injured during the riot. That was too much to take. The surviving hostages and the relatives of those who had died piled on the pressure, and finally in 2001 Governor George Pataki announced a new inquiry into the events at Attica in September 1971. The "Forgotten Victims" finally got a chance to tell their stories and explain the impact the riot had had on their lives. In 2005 an award of $12 million was announced, to be split between the survivors and bereaved.

The legal saga of the Attica riots hasn't quite ended, though. It's likely that all the compensation payments have now been made, but there are many unanswered questions. Were there other reasons why Governor Rockefeller refused to go to the prison? Did the State Police conceal or destroy photos of the gunshot wounds that killed so many hostages? Was there a cover-up to conceal the identities of the troopers who fired the fatal shots? Former State Supreme Court judge Bernard Meyer submitted a 570-page report on the riot in 1975. Only one of the three volumes was ever released; in 1981 the New York Supreme Court ordered the other two to be permanently sealed. In 2013 Attorney General Eric Schneiderman asked for the full report to be made public. If that happens then, perhaps, the full story will be revealed at last.

Chapter 7: Legacy

The events at Attica from September 9-13 1971 were a shocking blow to the New York State correctional system. The budget had been neglected for years and now that neglect had blown up in the government's face. Because journalists had been allowed in to the negotiations the siege had played out in public, and the people had been given a startling look inside the penal system. What they'd seen didn't look good and it added momentum to the calls for reform. Training for corrections officers was improved and more money was allocated for inmate welfare. When the damage was repaired B Block, the most heavily damaged, was rebuilt as an "honor block" where inmates could be reassigned as a reward for good behavior - the new cells are 50 percent larger and have cooking facilities.

One of the most important legacies of the Attica riot is a changed approach to dealing with prison uprisings. The carnage in D Yard that day finally convinced people that a frontal assault should only be considered as a last resort, and other approaches have to be exhausted first. In May 1991 prisoners at Southport Correctional Center, another New York prison, took three guards hostage. The authorities negotiated patiently and even granted demands for a TV interview. It worked; the inmates surrendered and the hostages were released unharmed.[xxi] In July that year convicts in Baltimore, MD grabbed two guards, but in 23 hours were talked into letting them go.

Whenever there's been a prison riot or hostage situation since 1971 the state governor has been on the scene, to negotiate, coordinate the response and present the state's side of the story to the media. Decades later many people still blame Rockefeller, who died in 1979, for the bloody ending of the Attica siege. By isolating himself at Pocantico Hills Rockefeller had denied himself first-hand knowledge of the situation. He had also angered the inmates, who had specifically asked for him and felt he was ignoring them. Rockefeller had legitimate security concerns - the danger of the governor walking into a yard controlled by 1,300 rioting criminals was obvious - but his failure to even travel to Attica just inflamed the situation. Most observers now believe he should have gone there early in the siege, and certainly before he authorized Oswald to go ahead with the assault.

Could Attica happen again? That's hard to say. American prisons are still tough places. They're overcrowded - the USA jails more of its people than any other nation, more than India and China combined. More than one American man in every 100 is currently in jail. With money short and budgets once more being cut that means overcrowding. The conditions in many prisons aren't as bad as Attica was in the distant summer of 1971, but in an age when people have much higher expectations about their quality of life they're still grim enough to cause real discontent. On the other hand the political climate has changed. Many of the civil rights issues that set U.S. cities on fire have been resolved; racism is still a problem but nowhere near as common as it was 42 years ago. The recent wars in Iraq and Afghanistan attracted plenty of opposition, but nothing on the scale of Vietnam. The Black Panther Party has faded into the history books and its surviving members share a lecture circuit with the ageing law professors who're all that remain of the Weather Underground. Whatever resentments smolder on in America's jails the fire of communist revolution isn't among them. Of course it's hard to predict what will happen in the pressure cooker atmosphere of a cellblock, so another major riot *could* erupt, but thanks to what was learned in upstate New York over those five days in 1971 we can hope the outcome will be far less bloody.

Bibliography

[i] The New York Times, March 11, 1991, *Obituaries: Russell Oswald*
http://www.nytimes.com/1991/03/11/obituaries/russell-oswald-82-prison-chief-in-new-york-during-attica-siege.html
[ii] BlackPast.org, *Attica Prison Riot (1971)*
  http://www.blackpast.org/?q=aah/attica-prison-riot-1971
[iii] Democrat and Chronicle, *Attica Prison Riot: Memories Strong After 40 Years*

http://www.democratandchronicle.com/section/ATTICA/Attica-Prison-Riot
[iv] Perkins, Margo V. *Autobiography As Activism: Three Black Women of the Sixties*. University Press of Mississippi. Jackson,2000. p. 5
[v] Attica Task Force Public Hearing, May 9, 2002*, Written statement of Thomas Fargo*

http://www.albany.edu/talkinghistory/attica/forgottensurvivors/FS5092002.pdf
[vi] PBS: American Experience, *Attica Prison Riot*

http://www.pbs.org/wgbh/americanexperience/features/general-article/rockefellers-attica/
[vii] Attica Task Force Public Hearing, May 10, 2002*, Testimony of Ron Kozlowski*

http://www.albany.edu/talkinghistory/attica/forgottensurvivor

s/FS5102002.pdf

[viii] Attica Task Force Public Hearing, May 9, 2002, *Written statement of Thomas Fargo*

http://www.albany.edu/talkinghistory/attica/forgottensurvivors/FS5092002.pdf

[ix] Attica Task Force Public Hearing, May 9, 2002, *Testimony of Elmer Huehn*

http://www.albany.edu/talkinghistory/attica/forgottensurvivors/FS8122002.pdf

[x] Attica Task Force Public Hearing, May 9, 2002, *Testimony of John Stockholm*

http://www.albany.edu/talkinghistory/attica/forgottensurvivors/FS5092002.pdf

[xi] Contra Costa Times, May 6, 2013, *Inmate convicted of Attica murder is found dead*
   http://www.contracostatimes.com/breaking-news/ci_23183135/inmate-convicted-attica-murder-is-found-dead

[xii] Attica Task Force Public Hearing, May 10, 2002, *Testimony of Ron Kozlowski*

http://www.albany.edu/talkinghistory/attica/forgottensurvivors/FS5102002.pdf

[xiii] Attica Task Force Public Hearing, May 10, 2002, *Testimony of Ron Kozlowski*

http://www.albany.edu/talkinghistory/attica/forgottensurvivors/FS5102002.pdf

[xiv] Attica Task Force Public Hearing, May 9, 2002, *Testimony of Royal T. Morgan*

http://www.albany.edu/talkinghistory/attica/forgottensurvivors/FS8132002.pdf

[xv] PBS, American Experience, *Attica Prison Riot*

http://www.pbs.org/wgbh/americanexperience/features/general-article/rockefellers-attica/

[xvi] Attica Task Force Public Hearing, May 9, 2002, *Testimony of Mary Stockholm*

http://www.albany.edu/talkinghistory/attica/forgottensurvivors/FS5092002.pdf

[xvii] Attica Task Force Public Hearing, May 9, 2002, *Testimony of Malcolm Bell*

http://www.albany.edu/talkinghistory/attica/forgottensurvivors/FS7302002.pdf

[xviii] Time Magazine, September 27, 1971, *War at Attica: Was There No Other Way?*
   http://www.time.com/time/magazine/article/0,9171,910027-7,00.html

[xix] Attica Task Force Public Hearing, May 10, 2002, *Testimony of Ron Kozlowski*

http://www.albany.edu/talkinghistory/attica/forgottensurvivors/FS5102002.pdf

[xx] Attica Task Force Public Hearing, May 9, 2002, *Testimony of Malcolm Bell*

http://www.albany.edu/talkinghistory/attica/forgottensurvivors/FS7302002.pdf

[xxi] Los Angeles Times, September 8, 1991, *Legacy of Deadly Attica Riot Is Nonviolence*
   http://articles.latimes.com/1991-09-08/news/mn-2845_1_prison-riot

Made in the USA
Las Vegas, NV
20 April 2022